emergency room wrestling

the dirty poet

Words Like Kudzu Press
State of Mind
2011

ISBN 978-0-9753862-1-7

Cover photo: Flexi, 2010

Words Like Kudzu Press
http://www.etsy.com/shop/EyeScorpion
eyescorpion@gmail.com

for the tortured genius

work is work, i'd say
i'm sorry, she'd say
then we'd laugh

hospitals exist; misery is real
this book is imagination
driving a lamborghini of experience

Dirty Poet Vs. The World

A few months ago The Dirty Poet and I were hanging out at the aptly named Beauty Bar on 14th Street in Manhattan, me staring drunkenly into my scotch and soda, and he happily handing out poems on yellow slips of paper with titles like *hail the cocksman, death and destruction on a friday night,* and *serial killer* to wary bar patrons. Somehow, the bartender was less than impressed. He told me, "I don't know what you or your friend are up to, but we can't have that in here." The Dirty Poet and I got out of the bar, but it left a bitter taste. I thought to myself this is what's wrong with America; the disparity in income and lifestyle between the richest Americans and everyone else grows exponentially on a monthly basis, our involvement in a seemingly unwinnable war for the greater part of the decade drags on interminably, and blowhards like Rush Limbaugh, Sarah Palin and Glenn Beck are taken seriously as political theorists. This is accepted as the status quo and allowed to continue with barely a murmur raised in protest, while somehow a writer handing out free poems to drunks is viewed as a threat. Unbelievable.

These poems are an antidote to what ails us. While the debate on healthcare rages on, these poems bring us into the belly of the beast, exploring the chaos, trauma and occasional small triumphs of daily life in the emergency room of a big city hospital. At times, it feels as if we are trapped in Dante's seventh circle of hell and we find ourselves gasping for breath. Fittingly, The Dirty Poet hails from New Jersey. In a manner comparable to Jersey state poet emeritus William Carlos Williams, the poems in this collection focus on details of life and work in the medical field. While The Dirty Poet does not completely adhere to Williams' famous dictum, "no ideas but in things," these poems are imagistic by nature, gritty in detail, yet quite human in their poignancy. Like the work of another Jersey bard, Bruce Springsteen, the work is written from a decidedly working class point of view. But unlike "the Boss's" persona, the speaker in these poems is 100% authentic. While the resolution of these poems is often death (and sometimes worse), our poet/protagonist carries on with a Sisyphean determination that is downright heroic in the face of impending doom. Morbid, yes, but there is an exuberance that rings through these verses which makes us appreciate living all the more.

I've known the Dirty Poet for a long time and his poetry and prose have consistently earned my admiration. *Emergency Room Wrestling* is a small sample of The Dirty Poet's wares, but we get a taste of his passions; work, death, beer, music and sex. The free verse flows with an understated dark humor told in a conversational, skeptical matter of fact voice. There is a musicality to these poems that helps make the subject matter bearable:

> the room looks like jimmy's bar after our christmas party
> littered with every device known to respiratory science
> but the tube doesn't want to go past the vocal chords
> *fuck!*

These poems offer us a choice, we can laugh, or we can cry. I choose to laugh. The Dirty Poet, what a pisser.

--Danny Shot

Meeting The Dirty Poet: A Preface

I found him in the Bowery Poetry Club, the first time I returned to New York since I'd moved away. It started as a query about the vegan sandwiches, but soon we were thick in a conversation about Allen Ginsberg, Alexander Berkman, *The East Village Eye*, Hudson County, Hoboken music clubs, Jandek, Andy Warhol, *The Evergreen Review*, and Maggie Dubris.

Eventually I learned that he was a hospital worker for a living-- an ER attendant--and had been for decades. This piqued my interest on a different level, as I'd been around medical culture all my life. Through my doctor father, I'd watched a progression from house calls and payments in venison and firewood, to insurance greed that kept my dad at the office later and later and made him cease to recommend the profession to his children, to new hospitals as Big Business and insurance policies that attempted to reduce visits with his patients to a mere 6 minutes. I grew up with a house full of drug-company freebies that got bigger and bigger: pens and post-it notes from hemorrhoid remedies, keychains announcing blood thinners, calculator-rulers advertising indigestion solution, a pill-shaped telephone mimicking a relief for acid reflux. At work, my dad was inundated with drug reps wooing the whole office staff with filet mignon lunches, or offering the doctor and his wife a free trip to Hawaii if he could hook 20 patients on a certain medicine.

Meanwhile, as a temp secretary at a research hospital, I'd once transcribed dictation from a top physician about a future "hospital company" that would be owned by the doctors for all the wrong reasons. Through friends and coworkers, I'd watched psychology go from talk therapy to mood meds, and expand from adults-mainly to children-often. I saw other friends fall into debt and fear from uninsured, unexpected medical emergencies. More recently, I'd heard through my father about "boutique practices," where well-to-do patients pay a high monthly fee to have their doctor on retainer 24/7. To me, the changes in medicine in my lifetime seemed all at once astounding, pharmaceutical-based, profit-driven, and part of an ever-widening class divide.

So, I was curious. I wanted to ask The Dirty Poet to tell me what went on inside the hospital, what changes had he seen, what insights? Who came into the ER, and who got out alive? As a critical thinker, how did he view The Hospital, and what did America in the 21st Century look like from the POV of an Emergency Room? What were the class dynamics, the gender tensions, the work relations? He was very cool as he conveyed that he didn't want to talk Hospital on his day off, but he told me, "I'll send you some poems." I believed him.

Lucky for me, the poems he sent me, a fine selection of which became EMERGENCY ROOM WRESTLING, answered my curiosity exactly, and my questions mostly. The POV of The Dirty Poet's ER is more timeless than timely, with the cycles of Life and Death hinging on choices made in a split second. Or does The Dirty Poet, in fact, capture something essential about the 21st Century: Its aggression, its entitlement, its anxiety; its stress, its relentless pace; its dance between technology and humanity; its service economy and the increasing hours spent at our jobs, waiting on the hapless, the helpless, the injured, and the impatient. As one Dirty Poet image puts it so clearly, "wall-to-wall patients gasping for air."

--Karen Lillis

you think *you* need a beer

you think *you* need a beer — i'm trapped in a hospital room
propping up a 400 pound naked man
                       who's been screaming for two days
he's got necrotizing fasciitis — flesh-eating bacteria —
                  of the crotch
and i'm helping three nurses reinsert his rectal trumpet
which has blared repulsive music all over the sheets
how do you let necrotizing fasciitis devour your scrotum?
did he act like most men — ignore it, hoping it would go away?
well it went away — the crotch, not the bacteria
and how the hell do you get to be 400 pounds?
do you wake up one day and say
                  i think these pants make me look fat?
oh no — the rectal trumpet popped out again
there she blows

must have been a full moon in that unit

there was debate whether the crack pipe
had been between her butt cheeks
or all the way up her ass
that was when the police picked her up last night
now she was on a ventilator in room #7 of the trauma ICU
bucking like an engine with bad timing
better pull the tube before she takes off, said the nurse
so i yanked it
half an hour later the patient asked me, *do i look bad?*
not too bad, i said
bitch hit me in the head with a weight, she croaked
well you look fine, i said
considering
forty-five minutes later she was cursing out the nurses
i hear them bitches laughing at me
who are they to judge me?
who indeed?
she ripped out her i.v.
i'm getting the fuck out of this hospital
going to summerville where they know how to treat a patient
i observed the doctor whispering to her as i passed by
on my way into room #9
where i found a mexican standoff
the patient had the nurse by the hair
let go of me, she said
he wouldn't
i grabbed his arm and tried to pry open his fingers
couldn't do it
i went around the bed and he punched me
stop it, we both whined gutlessly
the doctor came in the room
and separated nurse from patient
pull the tube, he told me
that's what i came in to do, i said
but there's no way i can do it if he's punching me
pull it anyway
okay, i said, *i need you to hold his arms*

four people jumped in and i extubated him
two minutes later he was peaceful as a puddle
as i left the room i heard *your patient's dead*
from gina, my preposterously hot fellow therapist
referring to the guy in room #8
wow, that was fast
i was going to snuff him myself
by chopping him from the ventilator
(family instructions)
but i'd been distracted by rooms 7 and 9
oh well
time to pack up a patient in #6 for a 3-hour MRI
he'd tripped down concrete stairs
while carrying two dogs, one in each arm
the dogs were ok, he broke the fall with his head

sure shot

as these things go, it's a happy ending
he tried shooting his girlfriend in the face
the gun jammed so he turned it around
aimed it under his chin and pulled the trigger
surprise -- it unjammed
the bullet tore through the mouth
and exited the left eye, missing the brain entirely
and even though he arrested thrice
before we got a breathing tube in
a week later we're shuffling him out of intensive care
hey look, Sure Shot's leaving, i say to my partner jeff
to which he responds, *you mean Old Dead Eye*

wake up call

we eat well in the ER
someone's always bringing in food
i gorge on chili all of superbowl sunday
dozing in a chair in the break room
it's 4 pm and i've done nothing all day
no respiratory issues for the handful of patients
BEEP
27 yr male, shot x 2 in chest, x 1 in back
ETA 3 min
i hustle to the trauma bay
blasted like that, the man's gonna die
but maybe not
not if we keep him breathing and his heart beating
until he gets up to the OR
for the surgeons to work their voodoo
everything is set for whatever in this room
but this time we unpack anything useful
endotracheal tubes, chest tubes, CO_2 detector
i put a blade on the laryngoscope
anything that take seconds to set up
subtracts from the patient's chances for survival
gowned and gloved, i tie on a face shield
blood may be raining all over the room
the six people beside me similarly prepare
doctors, nurses, anesthesiologist
adrenaline is seething like a drum roll
he'll launch through the door any second
BEEP
patient went to st. sebastian
damn
traumus-interruptus
well, i think as i unglove and ungown
that woke me up

serial killer

there's one murderous tree
putting itself in front of every car
it's a serial killer
there's one crippled kid in the ICU
he's in every bed
one set of frantic parents pacing every hall
standing shellshocked in each room

it's a neat metaphor
the single kid and singular set of parents
when there's zillions of each
but i'd watch out for that son-of-sam tree

emergency room wrestling

he weighed in with a handful of ambien
and a liter of vodka
i win again

dead end

i'm going to tell you the saddest story i know
because it happened
he was big and handsome, just 22
an unrestrained passenger in a car crash
he suffered a traumatic brain injury
leaving him wide-eyed and gone in an ICU
yesterday the nurses shoveled him into a chair
mom and dad resumed their vigil
mom shaky and crying, dad boisterous
all their family superhighways
leading to this disastrous dead end
dad took his son's large, limp hand
and said *come on buddy, thumb wrestle*
i bet i can beat you
come on buddy, let's do it
let's thumb wrestle, let's go
his thumb hopeful in a hopeless world

another christmas story

the patient swings a large leg out of bed
> *hold it,* i say, *you must stay where you are*
> *you got in a car accident this morning*
> *you had a seizure while you were driving*
> *now you're in the hospital*

his leg remains on the ground
i gotta go to the bathroom
> *you have a catheter, sir*
> *just go ahead and let loose*

he looks down past the sheet covering his chest
a rubber snake hangs out of his schlong
who put that in there?
> silence for a moment; then the nurse speaks
> *i did*

he looks at her
are you trying to flirt with me?
> *no, i'm not*
> > *so you're all set,* i say

but what if i pee a lot?
> the nurse holds up the sack connected to his hose
> it's the size of a shopping bag

he relaxes – and then tenses
is it supposed to sting?
> *it can sting a little*

man
merry fucking christmas to me

express yourself

he was combative, strapped to the bed
but he could still express himself
he spit a tooth at his nurse
and there's plenty more
where that came from, bitch

STUBS!

ARE THEY STUBS?
i'm not sure, sir
ARE THEY STUBS?
he's been shouting this for two days
his teeth were broken during intubation
some are missing
ARE THEY STUBS?
i have no perspective
i can't tell what's left
ARE THEY STUBS?
i understand why you're upset, sir
i would be too
but it's not for me to say
ARE THEY STUBS?

healing the sick

i enter the room for a breathing treatment
the family surrounds the bed, praying
can you come back later?
oh, no problem
yeah, you better pray
pray that i come back
the next patient screams
when i put on the aerosol mask
you hurt me!
i'm sorry, ma'am
you're not sorry, she says, glaring
oh yes i am
sorry i came in the room

familiar

it's familiar
i've seen this before, many times
looks like *the evil dead* or *reanimator*
my sneakers tapdancing around blood
the poor patient
naked and white as frozen milk
it's real
but it doesn't seem real
nurses joking about lunch
as we surround the leaking body
who hasn't heard that she's doomed
seems like a movie
and now i'm on a coffee break

long division

10 a.m.
a patient arrests in the hall
flat on the floor, no pulse
chest compressions, intubation, first in the stomach
a great geyser of green bile shoots through the endotube
reintubated correctly, bagging, more chest compressions
then blood surges out the tube
the end

we return to the respiratory room
redividing treatments for 11 a.m. rounds
i'm short so steve says, *take woodrow white*

woodrow white, i say
i treated him last week

yeah, woodrow's been hanging out a while
he was with a doctor this morning
so i skipped his treatment

i forget what woodrow white looks like

woodrow white? says the third therapist in the room
you just saw him

oh shit

we're silent a second

i guess we better redivide again

toothless

old coot
trached, leering, making kissy faces
at the cute young speech therapist
he's a harmless old lech
no threat, just a joke
he's cute like a naughty kitty
and i'm standing by
ten years, a stroke and a bad shave
from being there in bed with him
toothless in every way
i'll be just as irrelevant to that chick
as i am not today

another terminal wean

the woman has three daughters
one has been a basketcase all week
now that the time has come
and i start withdrawing life support from mom
the nervous daughter says, *nothing's gonna happen*
in the next five minutes, is it?
i have time to go outside for a cigarette,
don't i?
ten people and a priest in the room
surrounding the mother
well, yes, something could happen
her blood pressure is a whisper
but the woman looks like she could use a cigarette
family and friends are used to her indulgence
go get a cigarette
of course she's gone for twenty minutes
she goes upstairs for a cup of coffee
easy to call her an asshole but a woman has needs
and what's the rush?

holy shit

heard about the doctor running for the hospital elevator?
the doors were closing so he stuck his head in
decapitated
which is shocking enough
but imagine the folks inside the elevator

death and destruction on a friday night

if this night doesn't make my hair grey…
down the hall a 17-year old girl car accident from last night
every time she's scanned her brains are still scrambled
next to her another motor vehicle collision
a 41-year old kept alive so his wife can extract sperm
then he'll be let go (black widow style)
across the aisle a 78-year old who fell off his bar stool
cracked his head and he's gonna be withdrawn too
death and destruction on a friday night
but i'm sweating with this guy i extubated and can't reintubate
he absolutely could use oxygen about now
we pulled him off the breathing machine
he crumped, the doctors argued
and now we're trying to put a tube back in
we paralyzed him, the bronchoscope failed
i have another but it takes a couple of minutes to set up
he's almost dead and he was far from dying when we began
and his family is right outside the unit
the room looks like jimmy's bar after our christmas party
littered with every device known to respiratory science
but that tube doesn't want to go past the vocal cords
fuck!

pistol-whip

he came in pistol-whipped in the head
21 year old white male
a smiling bloody gash above his ear like a crater on mars
we got him on the gurney and asked what happened
he looked up at us and wildly offered
i just got my ASS kicked

the nitric kid in #7

nitric oxide dilates the pulmonary arteries
more blood flow = better oxygenation
it can be the difference between breathing and not
you only crank up the nitric ventilator
when the shit hits the fan
the last nitric kid died spectacularly
this one held on five nights after i worked with him
he needed the gas
when i tried quashing it he crashed
but came up when i turned it back on
his haitian mom put the voodoo on me
for trying to wean him
if you touch that machine
you'll never see your wife and kids again
but turning it off is the only way
of determining its necessity
but he needs it, said dr. mom
and he did
although five nights later it wasn't enough

scrubs

it's surreal, watching *scrubs* in my scrubs
in the ER lounge with the nurse of my choice
beep - level 1 and four minutes later
i'm hovering over a biker
whose heart stopped as soon as he hit the cart
i don't blame you dude
who hasn't got drunk and rolled his motorcycle?
but you should have worn that helmet
bagging O2, switching off for chest compressions
his belly sloshing around the bed
psychic focus, pushing on his heart
trying to make it catch like a west coast chopper
screw the giants, we're the hottest team in town
doh!-- just gave it the kunihara
we lose the game and i'm back on the couch
just in time for the next episode of *scrubs*

hospitality

you can literally get away with murder at the hospital
patients die every day
but if you leave work for the therapist on after you
your ass is written up
you could kill one or two people a shift
but you better drain those water bottles

trainwrecks are imminent

that's how you know it's busy in the ER
we get a guy who ran over his toes with a lawn mower
but there's three more traumas stacked up behind him
trainwrecks are imminent
so we downgrade him out of the trauma bay
he's no code one, says the doc calling the shots
get him and his toes out of here

human nature

let me ask you

you're sitting in a hospital room
visiting a friend or mother or son in a critical care bed
an alarm is triggered, an ominous warning
you nervously step outside looking for a nurse
you tell the nurse *there's something beeping*
the nurse comes inside and fixes the occluded line
you nitpick about the time it took
you question procedures as the nurse is doing them
advocating for the patient
the squeaky wheel gets the grease, right?
yeah but guess what
the nurse doesn't want to come in the room anymore
whether you're in there or not
the vitals will still be monitored
but other patients suddenly need more attention
and by the way
every time you ask me if i washed my hands
(like the posted signs advise you to ask)
i think: if you're that worried about infection
i'll just stay out of the room; that much less exposure
that means painful bedpan delay for your loved one
or lying in filth a little longer
waiting thirsty minutes for that sip of water
staying in one excruciating position half an hour more

so have you done your friend or mother or son a favor?

hail the cocksman

1.

four months ago
the i-phone in his chest
told him he was bad
too much masturbation
he should commit suicide
but he held off
on tuesday afternoon however
the i-phone in his chest
told him to take an x-acto knife
and slice off the evil appendage
plus one testicle for interest
which he did
we spent tuesday night
harvesting veins from the testicle
using them to sew his schlong
back in its place of honor
then
just in case his day wasn't tough enough
we brought out the leaches

2.

now it's three weeks later and he can't breathe
he's strapped to a prone bed
hanging upside down eighteen hours a day
his pecker is black as an old banana
scheduled to be clipped
in a minor bedside surgery
unless it falls off by itself

rock on

folks like to drink
folks like to drive
sometimes there are consequences
sometimes not
this fellow tied to the bed
screaming like ronnie james dio
his DTs have been rumbling for two days
now the storm has hit
and it's a tsunami
when he came to the hospital after the accident
he was so wasted he asked *was anyone else in the car?*
only your dead wife, dude
no one told him this
but he saw it on the news that night
which was last night
and today he's sweating and screaming
carrying on like a rock star

intelligent chart design

the doctor knocked out the old lady's tooth
during a difficult intubation
gave a yank when he should have finessed
they put the tooth in a specimen bag
and inserted it in the chart
damn
we're gonna need bigger charts
if they have to hold body parts

brains

let's call him brains
he shot his wife twice in the face with a .45
then put it in his mouth and blew out the back of his head
which saved his life; his brains could pour out the hole
as opposed to swelling against his skull and imploding
he weighs 465 pounds, unstoppable until last night
he has 15 children; the woman he shot was one of the mommies
she'd been married to his brother
             and had screwed his other brother
when i get to the room a teenage girl is holding his hand
she says she's his niece (*you know*
             this is an appalachian romance)
she's crying and pregnant and before she goes out for a cigarette
she says he's a teddy bear and something must have happened
when his family shows up they have no idea who she is
it's all about the tattoos, all about the love
f.u.c.k. scrawled on knuckles; on the other arm
             a leering death-head
and on his chest, prison tats of hearts with fluttering wings
we drag him to radiology and i bag him for an hour
admiring those tats while his brains leak some more
he's gonna die but the question is should his children see him
with those brains coming out his eyeballs
             or should they forego the closure
it's a decision that must be made soon, in fact tonight
cause by tomorrow morning it's a moot point

wrong

in the surgical intensive care unit
the therapist peeks in on an old man with an oxymizer
a plastic contraption that makes efficient use of pure oxygen
you strap it under your nostrils
hey, groucho wants his nose back
the old coot chuckles weakly as the therapist
steps back to the hall and tells me
patients love it when you joke with them
they're all scared of dying
and figure you wouldn't joke with someone dying
how wrong they are
and that expression no one ever died laughing?
wrong again

in the psych hospital

working in the psych hospital
giving breathing treatments
to a man with half a face
the left half
he blew off the right half with a pistol
a botched suicide
the gun bucked or his hand flinched
or both
he fucked up dying as he fucked up living
and we have to pick up the pieces

morning report

it was 7 a.m.
time for morning report
i looked over my list of treatments
oh no, mr. branco

a derelict with the nastiest of manners
branco has the doctors in a half nelson
they wrote for breathing treatments every two hours
giving him time to go downstairs for a smoke
he's been driving everyone nuts for months

branco, said steve
a therapist for eighteen years
i walked in there the other day
and he was sucking his own dick

what?

he was sucking his own dick

no

oh yeah, he was
i asked him if he was getting anything out of that pipe

he is a lanky bastard, i conceded
and it does get dull in the hospital

i didn't really believe he sucked his own dick
but every time i entered his room for a treatment
it was a party

acidosis

she was the hottest nurse
body too thin, tight oversize tits
black hair, nervous eyes, pretty face
just *smoking*
the patient came in
first detail reported by EMS
his pants were around his ankles
most likely found down taking a dump
but maybe something sexual
we took him to scan
i stood next to the hottest nurse and said
well, now i know how to begin my report
his pants around his ankles
she said, *yeah that was the most relevant fact*
i said, *it usually means acidosis*
and she laughed

mr. ziegler

i walked in on mr. ziegler
he'd fallen out of bed
he was like a peanut-butter-and-jelly sandwich
smeared with shit and blood
he was still kicking so i grabbed some gloves
i said *don't move*
and called to the staff in the hall
patient fell out of bed
he was embarassed by his helplessness
mortified by his filth
i would be too
we hauled him back in bed
the nurses hosed him down
i gave him a breathing treatment
and getting old continued to suck

an easy night

last night i got my ass kicked in trauma
juggling bodies, crises, bloody tracheas
wall-to-wall patients gasping for air
tonight's different; seems like a light evening
i'm rendering treatments to acceptably ill folks
go in this room here, full of family
it's a cheerful scene
the old fellow seems fine
oh shit
no toes on either foot

sympathy

the woman came in assaulted
her boyfriend had come home and belted her in the head
what a bastard we all said as we awaited her arrival in the ER
within 20 minutes four security guards were strapping her down
using the 4-point leather restraints kept for drunk maniacs
which she was
listen nigger she said to the largest white man in the room
get your motherfucking hands off me
the amused doctors ordered propothol
as the petite nurse prepared it, the patient said
oh you bitch, if you stick that needle in me
you're never gonna see your kids again
she went down seething
when i get these straps off you're all fucking dead
i remember everyone's face
we all felt the same thing
sympathy for the boyfriend

the reality of finality

he stroked out after heart surgery
and now his time has come
he's way too young for this
and the family has been wailing for two days
understandable
but we actually don't see much of that
everyone's too dazed by the reality of finality
when the breathing tube comes out
his engine sputters into motion
it's a bottomless well of secretions
each muddy gasp promoting
an accompanying wave of horror
from the family in the room
i stick in a nasal trumpet
i stick in an oral airway
i stick a suction catheter up his nose
triggering a vast bubble of yellow bile out his mouth
step back! i shout
the room screams
i put the catheter down his oral airway
a first for me, and for the room in general
everyone's in shock
i'm going to do this again, i announce
i know there's a lotta bad stuff coming out
but i think it helped
i do it again in technicolor
and step back myself
the wife hugs his tattooed neck
the mother on his right shoulder
the knockout nurse is in tears
she should have snowed him more
as she's angrily reminded by the physician
this is the most horrible thing i've ever gone through
she says outside the room
i give words of chilly comfort
with all their carrying on

he couldn't have gone quietly
it had to be this way

ghosts

in the ICUs people are so fucked up
so gone, ventilated, sedated, deficit
that they're ghosts lying there
only afterwards, if they survive
are they reborn as people
strolling through the units
thanking medicos they don't remember

harley

when the sign above a patient's bed
says *call me harley*
you don't have to ask

rectum?

there's nobody here from the press, is there?
why do you ask, doctor?
because last time, there was
a few minutes later she's quoting henny youngman
rectum? damn near killed him
harsh humor for the circumstance
we're in the operating room
ready to pull the plug on some poor soul
i have the honor of being the plug-puller
once i perform my soliloquy
the surgeons will carve out his organs
faster than *flight of the bumblebee*
there's a couple of small buckets on the table behind me
half full of ice and labeled *left kidney, right kidney*
usually this process is more organic
i've withdrawn support from lots of unlucky bastards
but they're gone already
this guy is damaged for sure, but he's not gone
he's here
and then he's not

afterwards i'm on a stool at my local ice box
a couple of beers to cut the grease in my soul
although if i drank after every stressful day of work
i'd be swimming laps in a wavepool of yuengling

unlikely

as i sit on this fellow's legs at bergen pines psychiatric
while doctors dither about whether to give him haldol
i keep checking my phone for love
but it's like expecting a text from my cat

done deal

they're dying to get in this unit
and dying to get out
bed 7 is still empty
the patient never made it out of the OR
but bed 8 is quite occupied
the "kids" are agonizing over a "choice"
but there is no choice
pops (age 78) fell and flattened his brain
it's a done deal, all over
the only decision is when to walk away
any options are not in human hands
and here's the nurse as i write this
looks like the "kids" made their "choice"
she's pumping the morphine
and i'm yanking the curtain
it's a done deal

why a career in respiratory therapy?

hey, people have to breathe
why shouldn't i get a few bucks?

worst case scenario

imagine this poem stretching on for the next six pages
that's how long my morning was

monitoring a diabetic patient injected with barium
her eyes wide but responding to nothing
no legs and ventilator-dependant for the past four years
a jumbo sack of tragedy -- a worst case scenario

i was paired with two young radiologists
charming, with fantastic matching asses
they gave a fresh coat of paint to this house of horror
i had a spire of desire for six hours

even as i stared at my legless worst case scenario
a long, sick, delicious morning

one, two

the patient wanted to know
why she couldn't keep her advair bedside
don't you trust us to count to two?
one puff in the morning, one at night?

i told her sorry, but no
people are not at their sharpest in the hospital
i have to keep track of what you take
and when you take it

i pocketed the advair and moved on to the next patient
who'd assured me five minutes earlier
that she was awake enough to use a mouthpiece
for her breathing treatment; when i reentered the room
she had the drug aerosol stuck in her ear

okay?

believe it

well i tell you
in the good old days he'd been a cardiologist
right here at the hospital
more recently he'd been vegetating in a nursing home
until he started poking every eyeball he could reach
so they stashed him in bergen pines psychiatric
until he had convulsions
so now he's back home in the hospital
on the wrong end of a breathing tube
and his wife has parkinson's
she's shivering in the corner
deciding whether to withdraw support
and their son died last month
i tell you
the trend isn't good

yet i believe a moment exists
a dimension, a reality
where he's still a cardiologist
his son is young and playing first base
he and his wife watch the game in lawn chairs
on a little league saturday morning in may
the boy hits a double and steals third
the sun shines like god smiling
they have money and love and health and happiness
and a future of limitless good fortune

i believe it
why not

About the Author

The Dirty Poet was born in Northern New Jersey during the Cold War. His poems have appeared in numerous publications and have been recited on many stages. *Emergency Room Wrestling* is his first book.

About Words Like Kudzu Press

Kudzu is a type of ivy, originally from Japan, which grows rampantly in the Southern region of the United States. Considered by most a deadly weed, kudzu is a beautiful deep-green plant which could cover a building, say an eyesore of a modern building, in three days. (Consider it.)

Words Like Kudzu Press is interested in the power of words and the poetic to destroy and recover.

WLK has been publishing poetry and experimental prose by women and other outsiders since 2000. It began in an apartment in Greenpoint, Brooklyn with the underground novel, *i, scorpion: foul belly-crawler of the desert.*

www.ingramcontent.com/pod-product-compliance
Lightning Source LLC
Chambersburg PA
CBHW032216040426
42449CB00005B/629